PASSPORT TO

UNITED STATES

Keith Lye

Watts Books
London/New York/Sydney

This edition 1993

First published in Great Britain by
Watts Books
96 Leonard Street
London EC2A 4RH

First published in Australia by
Franklin Watts Australia
14 Mars Road
Lane Cove
NSW 2066

UK ISBN: 0 7496 1135 9

Editors: John Clark
Hal Robinson
Design: Edward Kinsey
Illustrations: Hayward Art Group
Series Consultant: Keith Lye

Photographs: Chris Fairclough Colour Library 5T, 6T, 8B, 9 all, 12 all, 13 all, 16 all, 17 all, 18 all, 19B, 20 all, 21 all, 22 all, 24 all, 25 all, 29 all, 30T, 34 all, 35T, 38 all, 39B, 41B; Ford Motor Company 33T; Hutchison Picture Library 10B, 31B, 35B; Kobal Collection 33B, 40, 41T; Keith Lye 6B, 30B; NASA 32T; Popperfoto 42T, 43, 44T; Rex Features 32B; Frank Spooner Library 44B, 45T; USDA 28 all; Western Americana 42B; Ken Windsor 11B; Zefa Picture Library 7T, 7B, 8T, 10T, 19T, 22B, 31T, 39T, 45B.

Front cover: Bruce Coleman Limited; ZEFA (inset).

Phototypeset by Keyspools Limited
Colour reproduction by Hong Kong Graphic Arts
Printed in Belgium

Contents

Arctic Ocean
Brook Range
Bering Strait
CANADA
Yukon R.
ALASKA
Range
Mt McKinley
Alaska
Anchorage
Seward
Juneau
Kodial I.
Aleutian Islands
CANADA
L. Superior
Great Lakes
L. Huron
Seattle
Spokane
Portland (Oregon)
Snake R.
Boise
Rocky Mountains
Missouri R.
Great Plains
Coast Ranges
Reno
Sacramento
San Francisco
Great Basin
Mt. Whitney
Great Salt Lake
Salt Lake City
Colorado R.
Las Vegas
Grand Canyon
Los Angeles
San Diego
Phoenix
Tucson
Denver
Colorado Springs
Albuquerque
El Paso
Rio Grande
Duluth
St. Paul
Minneapolis
L. Michigan
Milwaukee
Madison
Chicago
Detroit
Omaha
Lincoln
Des Moines
Indianapolis
Kansas City
Cincinatti
St. Louis
Louisville
Wichita
Tulsa
Oklahoma City
Red R.
Mississippi R.
Memphis
Little Rock
Nashville
Chattanooga
Atlanta
Birmingham
Jackson
Montgomery
Fort Worth
Dallas
Shreveport
Austin
Houston
New Orleans
Mobile
San Antonio
Corpus Christi
Portland (Main
L. Ontario
Rochester
Buffalo
Boston
Mountains
L. Erie
Cleveland
Pittsburgh
New York City
Philadelphia
Columbus
Baltimore
Washington DC
Richmond
Norfolk
Virginia Beac
Appalachian
Raleigh
Charlotte
Charleston
Jacksonville
Orlando
Tampa
Miami
BAHAMAS
Scale 1:10,000,000
0 200 400 km
0 100 200 300 400 miles
Straits of Florida
Gulf of Mexico
MEXICO
CUBA
JAMAICA
BELIZE
Caribbean Sea
GUATEMALA
HONDURAS
NICARAGUA
Kaui
Nihau
Oahu
Honolulu
Molokai
Maui
Lanai
Hilo
Mauna Loa
Hawaii
Pacific Ocean
HAWAII

Introduction

The United States is the world's fourth largest country, both in area and population. It was founded on July 4, 1776, when 13 British colonies on the eastern seaboard of North America declared independence.

Today the nation consists of 50 states and the District of Columbia, an area set aside for the national capital, Washington. The 48 contiguous states occupy the southern part of North America, from Canada to Mexico. The two other states are Alaska, which was purchased from Russia in 1867 for $7.2. million, and Hawaii, which were annexed by the United States in 1898. Alaska and Hawaii achieved statehood in 1959.

The United States is a land of enormous scenic and climatic variety, with vast areas virtually empty of people neighbouring some of the world's greatest cities. The population, made up largely of immigrants and their descendants, is equally varied. Through hard work, initiative and invention, the people have exploited their country's tremendous natural resources, turning the United States into the world's richest and most powerful nation.

Above: About three out of every four people in the United States live in urban areas. The largest city is New York City.

Left: Monument Valley is in the Navajo Tribal Park on Utah's border with Arizona. It is thinly populated. The United States has many areas which are almost empty of people.

The land

Coastal plains border the eastern seaboard of the United States from Maine to Florida, while the broad Gulf Coastal Plain extends from Florida to Texas. Running through this plain is the Mississippi River, which reaches the Gulf of Mexico below New Orleans. An ancient mountain range, the Appalachians, extends from Alabama in the south to Maine in the northeast and on into Canada. West of the Appalachians are the interior plains, including the Great Lakes region and the broad prairies. The prairies, now largely agricultural, extend to the majestic Rocky Mountains, which began to rise in recent geological time (as early as 60 million years ago). The Rockies run from New Mexico northward into Canada and Alaska.

West of the Rockies lie the western plateaus, basins and ranges. The Columbia plateau was formed by ancient lava flows, whereas the Colorado plateau was raised up by earth movements. Cutting through it is the magnificent Grand Canyon.

Above: The scenic coasts of California are battered by Pacific Ocean waves.

Below: The Grand Canyon in Arizona is one of the world's finest natural wonders.

Left: Plains cover much of the central United States. Scott's Bluff, Nebraska, which can be seen from far away, was a landmark for pioneers crossing the plains.

Below: New England in the northeastern United States has warm summers and cold, snowy winters. The autumn foliage provides a magnificent spectacle.

In the Far West are the Pacific Ranges, including the Sierra Nevada, the Cascades and the Coast Ranges. The Cascades contain active volcanoes, such as Mount Saint Helens, which erupted in 1980. Lowlands include California's fertile Central Valley. California contains the San Andreas Fault, whose movements cause earthquakes. The Pacific ranges extend into Alaska and the Aleutian Islands. Alaska contains Mount McKinley, the highest peak.

Northern Alaska has a polar climate, with treeless tundra vegetation. By contrast, coniferous forests grow in the wet, cool states of Oregon and Washington, with mangrove swamps in subtropical Florida. The rainfall varies from the southwestern deserts, where Death Valley, California, has only 5 cm (2 inches) of rain a year, to Mount Waialeale, Hawaii, with about 1,230 cm (484 inches). The interior plains have an extreme dry, continental climate. The northeast has a cool maritime climate, while the southwest coast of California has a Mediterranean climate.

The people

The first people to settle in North America, around 25,000 or more years ago, came from Asia. They were the ancestors of the Native Americans (also called American Indians). They were followed by the ancestors of the Inuit (Eskimos), more than 10,000 years later.

While the Inuit stayed in the north, the descendants of the earliest Native Americans moved south, founding civilizations in Mexico, Central America and South America. In Canada and the United States, they were mainly hunters and farmers. In the 1490s, when Europeans arrived, they numbered about 1 million.

Contact with European settlers proved almost disastrous for the Indians. Wars and epidemics of European diseases to which the Indians lacked resistance caused many deaths. By 1900, the Indian population of the United States had fallen to 237,000. In 1990, the Native Americans numbered 1,952,234, or 0.8 per cent of the total population. About half of them live in areas called reservations.

Above: Mohave Indians live in the interior of California. They are one of many Native American groups.

Left: Large numbers of immigrants from Europe and Russia entered the United States through New York City in the 19th and 20th centuries. The city retains a multi-cultural character.

Left: Most black Americans are of African descent. About half live in the southeast. Most of the others live in cities in the north and west.

Below left: A Japanese American student in Boston. Americans of Asian descent also include Chinese, Filipinos and Vietnamese.

Far left: A sheriff in Maine. The sheriff, the chief law enforcement officer in most counties, is elected by the people.

Below: A Jewish American couple. Many Jewish immigrants settled in the United States in order to escape persecution in the lands of their birth.

The earliest settlers in what is now the United States were Spaniards. But of greater significance was the founding of the first British settlement at Jamestown, Virginia, in 1607, followed by the arrival of the Pilgrims in New England in 1620. In 1619, the first African slaves were introduced.

Today whites make up 80.3 per cent of the population and African Americans 12 per cent. A majority of the people are of European descent. Most of the early European settlers were English. Later immigrants came from France, Germany, Ireland, the Netherlands, Scandinavia and Scotland and, in the late 19th century, from eastern Europe and Russia. Spanish-speaking people, mainly from Cuba, Mexico and Peru, are classed as whites. Called Hispanic Americans, they numbered about 22,354,000 in 1990.

Asians have also entered the "melting pot" – a term often used to describe the United States. They include Chinese, Filipinos, Vietnamese, Koreans and Japanese.

Above: A hotel cashier in Connecticut, one of the six states of New England, an area once ruled by Britain.

Below: A student at Harvard University, the country's oldest institution of higher education.

Where people live

A hundred years ago, the United States was a mainly rural country, with the greatest densities of population in the northeast and Great Lakes regions. This pattern has been gradually changing. The populations of the West and the South have been expanding rapidly. The South and Southwest, especially the states of Florida, Texas, Arizona, Nevada and California, have been attracting people because of their pleasant climate. "Sunbelt" cities, such as Houston, Texas, and Phoenix, Arizona, offer increasing job opportunities.

By 1990, 77.5 per cent of the population of the United States lived in urban areas, ranging from great cities, with their towering skyscrapers, to small towns. These urban areas covered less than 2 per cent of the land. The region with the greatest population density lies between Boston, Massachusetts, and Richmond, Virginia. This region is often called a megalopolis – a huge, sprawling urban area. This "super-city" includes New York City, the country's biggest city. The second and third largest are Los Angeles-Long Beach and Chicago.

Above: In 1800, 95 out of every 100 Americans lived in rural areas. This part of Pennsylvania was settled by the Amish, a Protestant group from Switzerland.

Below: Many people live in small communities, such as this town in Colorado. Cars make it possible for people to live some distance away from their workplaces.

The last 40 years have seen many changes in the cities themselves. In 1950, 56 per cent of the urban population lived in central city areas, as compared with less than 30 per cent today. The shift to the suburbs has been made possible by the widespread use of cars.

The move to the suburbs is marked in the North. However, many inner-city areas have been repopulated by Hispanic Americans and African Americans from the poor rural South. These areas, which already suffered pollution and traffic jams, have become ghettos for the poor, unemployed and old. Another trend is the move of some city people into rural areas. But the majority of the rural population lives within daily commuting range of a city.

The capital, Washington DC, also has overcrowded slums occupied by African Americans, who make up about 70 per cent of its population. The city centre, however, contains many graceful historic monuments.

Above: St Louis, Missouri, is a major industrial city and inland port on the Mississippi River. Modern skyscrapers tower above older buildings.

Below: Washington DC, the national capital, contains many graceful and historic public buildings, such as the Capitol, where Congress makes laws.

New York City

The population of the metropolitan area of New York City in the 1990 census was about 18,807,000. This makes it one of the world's largest urban areas. It is the country's top financial, shipping, transportation, communications and cultural centre.

There are five boroughs. The smallest, the island of Manhattan, is the best known. Its dramatic skyline is punctuated by skyscrapers, such as the Empire State Building and the twin towers of the World Trade Center, the second highest building in the world after Chicago's Sears Tower. The other boroughs are Brooklyn, the Bronx, Queens and Staten Island.

The first settlement in New York was established on Manhattan Island by the Dutch in 1624. In 1626, the settlement's director general, Peter Minuit, bought Manhattan Island from the Indians for goods worth $24. The English took New Amsterdam, as it was called, during the wars between them and the Dutch in 1652–74 and renamed it New York.

Above: The Statue of Liberty stands on Liberty Island in New York Harbour. It was given to the United States by France in 1884.

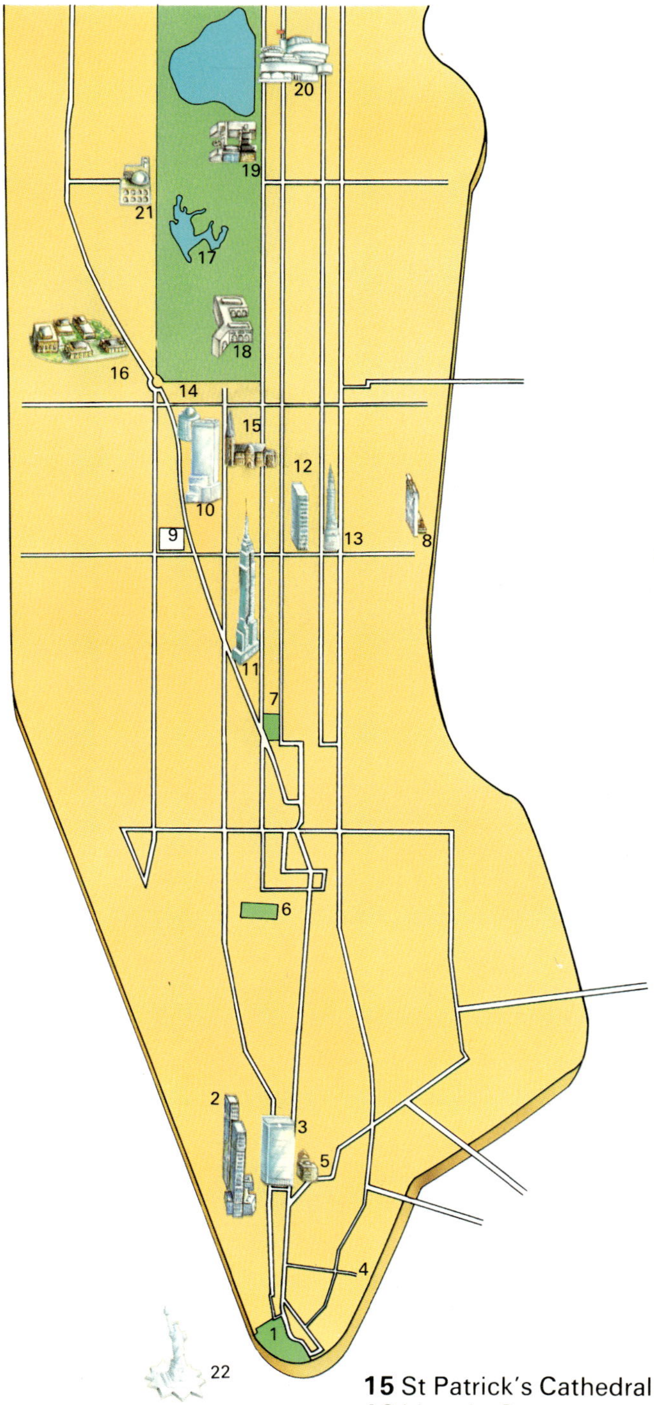

1 Battery Park
2 World Trade Center
3 Woolworth Building
4 Wall Street
5 City Hall
6 Washington Square
7 Madison Square Gardens
8 United Nations Building
9 Times Square (Broadway)
10 Rockefeller Center
11 Empire State Building
12 Pan Am Building
13 Chrysler Building
14 Carnegie Hall
15 St Patrick's Cathedral
16 Lincoln Center
17 Central Park
18 Zoo in Central Park
19 Metropolitan Museum of Art
20 Guggenheim Museum
21 Museum of Natural History
22 Statue of Liberty

Above: The skyline of lower Manhattan, dominated by the twin towers of the World Trade Center, is one of the world's most dramatic.

Five main groups make up four-fifths of New York City's population: African Americans, Irish, Italians, Jews and Puerto Ricans. Smaller groups include Chinese, Cubans, Germans and Poles. New York City was the gateway for millions of European immigrants. Their hope for a better life is symbolized by the Statue of Liberty in New York Harbour.

Wall Street, near the southern tip of Manhattan, is a famous financial centre. Nearby is Chinatown and the World Trade Center. Greenwich Village and SoHo are populated by actors, artists, writers and musicians. North again, where two well-known streets Broadway and Seventh Avenue intersect, is Times Square, heart of the theatre district. The United Nations Building overlooks the East River, while to the northwest is Central Park. Great museums include the Metropolitan Museum of Art, the Museum of Modern Art, the Guggenheim Museum and the American Museum of Natural History. The fine churches include St Patrick's Cathedral.

Below: The island of Manhattan, the smallest borough in New York City, faces problems of traffic jams and overcrowding.

Fact file: land and population

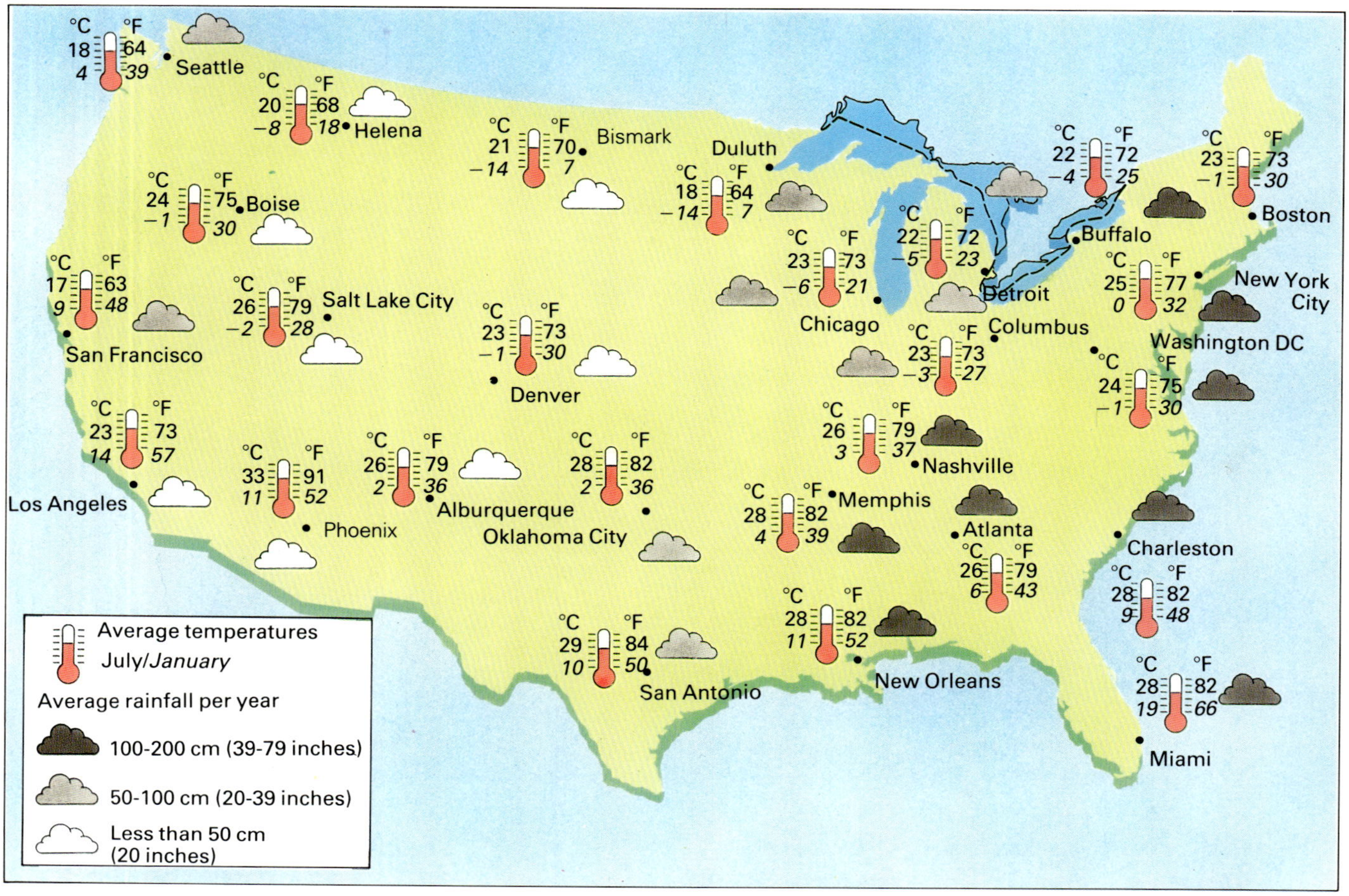

△ The climate of the United States

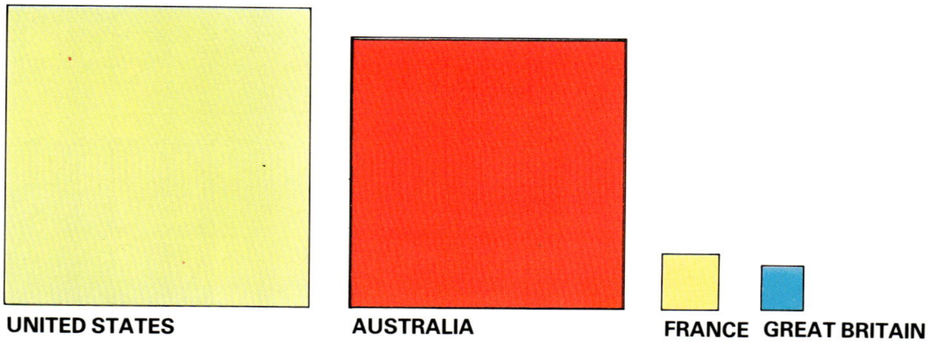

▷ **A land area comparison**
The USA is the world's fourth largest country. It is larger than Australia, nearly 5 times as large as Mexico, and over 38 times as large as the United Kingdom.

Key facts

Location: The 48 contiguous (or continental) states occupy that part of North America which lies roughly between latitudes 24°30′ North and 49° North, and longitudes 67° West and 124°45′ West. The 49th and largest state, Alaska, occupies the northwestern corner of North America. The 50th state, Hawaii, is a group of islands in the North Pacific Ocean.

Main parts: Besides the 50 states, the United States possesses various islands in the Caribbean Sea and the Pacific Ocean.

Area: 9,370,000 sq km (3,600,000 sq miles).

Population: 248,709,873 (1990 census).

Capital: Washington D.C.

Major cities (1990 populations):
- New York City (7,323,000)
- Los Angeles (3,485,000)
- Chicago (2,784,000)
- Houston (1,631,000)
- Philadelphia (1,586,000)

Official language: English.

Highest point: Mount McKinley, Alaska, 3,779 m (20,320 ft).

Lowest point: Death Valley, California, 86 m (282 ft) below sea level.

Longest rivers: Mississippi, 3,779 km (2,348 miles).

Largest lake: Lake Superior in the Great Lakes covers 82,103 sq km (31,700 sq miles), of which part is in Canada. The largest lake entirely within the United States is Lake Michigan, with an area of 57,757 sq km (22,300 sq miles).

△ **Where people live**
The proportion of people living in cities and towns in the United States is still increasing.

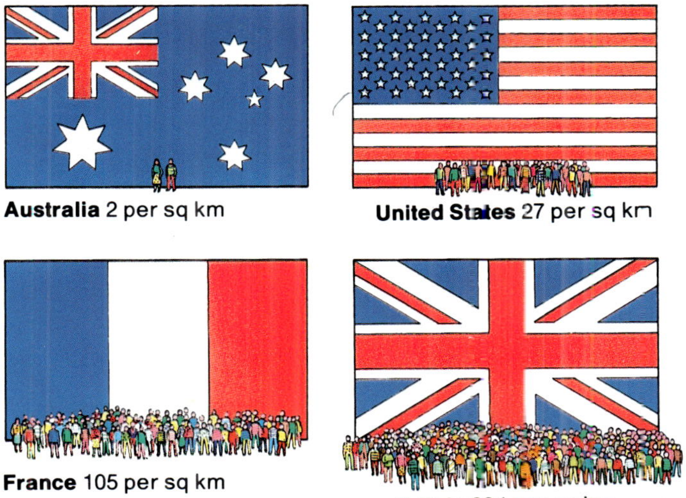

△ **A population density comparison**
The United States contains large areas that are virtually empty of people. As a result, the average population density is low by comparison with many other countries.

▽ **Major population centres and interstate highways**

Home life

In 1990, 70.8 per cent of households were occupied by families, while 25 per cent contained people living alone or with someone who was not a relative. The family remains important in American society, although it has been changing in character, partly because people have become increasingly mobile. Americans move an average of 13 times in a lifetime, often to find work or to get a better job. As a result, most Americans no longer live in extended family groups – that is, close to grandparents, aunts, uncles and other relatives. Instead most households contain only parents and children.

In cities, people live in rental apartments or condominiums (individually owned apartments) or in single-family houses. Six out of every seven homes have at least one room per family member. Although most Americans shop and cook for themselves, life is made easier by many domestic time-saving devices.

Above: Many people who work in central city areas live in pleasant suburbs. The picture shows Rye, a suburb of New York City.

Below: The television is a centre of attraction for children in the early evening after they have returned home from school.

American families are, on the average, among the most prosperous in the world. They enjoy, according to the Organization for Economic Cooperation and Development (OECD), the world's highest standard of living. In 1990, the average household consisted of 2.6 people and the average household income was $35,700. The average working week consisted of 41 hours, including overtime.

About 85 per cent of homes have a TV set and a car, while more than 50 per cent have two or more TV sets and cars. Cars play an important part in society with drive-in movies, restaurants and even banks.

Some families, such as those in crowded inner-city slums, are classed as poor. In 1990, a poor family was defined as any non-farming family of four with a total annual income of less than $13,359. Some 33.6 million people, including 10.7 per cent of whites and 31.9 per cent of African Americans, fell into this category. Poor whites included sizeable numbers of Hispanic Americans. Most Native Americans live below the poverty line.

Above left: Most American homes have well-equipped kitchens. The picture shows mother preparing a mixed salad, which is a regular part of the diet of most families.

Above: Children play games in the bedroom.

Below: Many suburban homes have spacious gardens where the family can relax on summer days.

Stores and shops

While small and medium-sized stores selling one main line of product, such as footwear, are found throughout the United States, the country has pioneered several other forms of selling, which are now copied in many countries. For example, since the early 1900s, chain stores have sold products at low prices because of bulk buying and the low operation costs. Much food is now sold by food-store chains. In the early 1980s, the leading food-store chain was Safeway Stores.

Department stores offer a wide range of goods under one roof, with each kind of merchandise in a separate department. Famous American department stores include Marshall Field in Chicago, R. H. Macy in New York City, and Nieman-Marcus in Dallas.

Department stores were developed in the late 19th century, whereas supermarkets date back only to the 1930s. The attraction of supermarkets is their convenience as well as their prices. They sell a wide range of food and drink, and many kinds of domestic products.

Above: A shopping complex in a city suburb is fronted by a large car park.

Left: Supermarkets carry a wide range of products, all attractively packaged.

Left: One of the best-known department stores in the United States is R. H. Macy in New York City.

Parking is an essential feature of the most recent development – the construction of shopping centres or malls. The size of these depends mainly on the size and economic conditions of the communities they serve.

The smallest shopping centres usually include a supermarket and a range of small or medium-sized specialty shops, with shoe repairs, laundry and other services. A community shopping centre, catering to 40,000 to 150,000 people, also contains one or more department stores. The largest regional centres include many other features, including medical centres, office space, restaurants, hotels, cinemas, apartment buildings and even churches. Special events, such as fashion shows and antique shows, are often held to attract customers. These large regional centres contain an open area for shoppers called a mall. Enclosed malls are heated in winter and air-conditioned in summer, making them pleasant places in which to shop.

Below: Modern malls provide a pleasant environment for shoppers. This enclosed mall is in White Plains, New York.

Cooking and eating

Most American kitchens are well equipped, with refrigerators and lots of electrical gadgets. To save time, many people buy prepared foods which can be quickly made ready for the table. On special holidays, families enjoy elaborate meals. For example, on Thanksgiving Day, the fourth Thursday in November, families gather for a turkey dinner with pumpkin pie in memory of the first Thanksgiving, celebrated by the Pilgrims at Plymouth in 1621.

The United States is known around the world for its inexpensive fast food, including hamburgers, sandwiches, pizzas, salad bars, and a great variety of ice cream. Fast food chains, such as McDonalds and Kentucky Fried Chicken, operate in many countries.

The United States also has many ethnic restaurants. Chinese, French, Italian and Mexican cooking are especially popular, but there are many other restaurants, including those serving Filipino, German, Greek, Japanese and Vietnamese dishes.

Above: Many Americans eat large breakfasts, including melon, fruit juice, fried sausages and bacon, scrambled eggs and toast with marmalade.

Below: Many American families are changing their eating habits and eating more fresh food, including salads, alongside traditional roasts.

Left: On a day out, families often eat at restaurants belonging to one of the major fast food chains.

Below: Pizzas are popular dishes at home and in restaurants. They were introduced by Italian immigrants.

Because of its great size and its climatic and ethnic variety, there are many special regional dishes. The northeast is known for such foods as Boston baked beans and Boston brown bread, and also New English clam chowder (a creamy stew made with clams and salt pork). The South is famed for grits (made with ground corn), Southern Fried Chicken, Maryland crabcakes, New Orleans jambalaya (made with chicken, crab, ham and prawns), and Texan chili con carne. Mid-Western dishes include bratwurst (sausage) from Wisconsin.

In recent years, many people have become increasingly concerned about their health and the fear of becoming overweight. Many are also concerned about food additives, which might be harmful to the body. As a result, an increasing number of people are changing their eating habits. Many are eating more fresh fruits, vegetables and whole-grain foods. "Health foods", including those grown without the use of chemical fertilizers and pesticides, are becoming more and more popular.

Pastimes and sports

Popular home leisure activities include such hobbies as gardening and collecting coins and stamps, watching television, listening to music and reading. Many families travel to recreational areas for day or weekend trips. Especially popular are the country's 50 national parks and other preserved areas, where people stay in hotels, tents, mobile homes and trailers.

Most Americans take part in sports, including bicycle riding, fishing, golf, hiking and hunting in wilderness areas, running, swimming, tennis, skiing and ice skating. The leading professional team sports are football, hockey, basketball and baseball.

Football, which non-Americans call American football to distinguish it from soccer, is played from autumn to spring. This exciting sport, which requires great skill and strategy, evolved in the mid-19th century from English rugby. The game is played at high school and college level, and professionally by teams in the National Football League.

Above: The United States has many spectacular national parks and other recreational areas. Mount Rushmore National Memorial, South Dakota, shows the heads of four presidents which have been cut into a granite cliff.

Left: Disney World, near Orlando, Florida, is one of the world's best-known amusement parks. Here visitors can meet such famous characters as Donald Duck. Another Disneyland is at Anaheim, near Los Angeles.

Above: Football is a team sport which originated in the United States.

Left: Basketball courts are common sights on many city playgrounds.

Below: Large crowds flock to watch professional baseball games. Millions more follow the sport on television, radio and through newspaper reports.

Hockey, which non-Americans call ice hockey to distinguish it from field hockey, is played between October and April. This fast game, involving two teams of six players on the ice, developed in Canada. North America's major professional hockey organization is the National Hockey League.

Basketball is played in winter and spring. It was invented in 1891 by Canadian-born James A. Naismith, who taught physical education in Springfield, Massachusetts. The National Basketball Association is the leading professional league.

Baseball evolved in the mid-19th century from the British game of rounders. There are two major leagues: the National League, founded in 1876, and the American League, founded in 1900. The pennant winners of these two leagues meet in the world series, which is followed on television and radio by millions of people.

News and broadcasting

In 1990, the United States had 1,626 daily newspapers, with a total circulation of 63 million. Because the United States is so large, there is no tradition of national newspapers, though some, such as the influential *New York Times*, the *Wall Street Journal*, the *Christian Science Monitor* and the *Los Angeles Times*, are available in large cities. However, using satellite technology, a full-colour daily newspaper called *USA Today* is now printed in several regional centres from material that is circulated electronically. Electronic distribution of news is now used by several newspapers.

News magazines with wide circulation include *Newsweek* and *Time*, though the magazines with the highest circulation are *Reader's Digest*, *TV Guide* and the *National Geographic*, all of which have circulations of more than 10 million.

In 1991, there were about 520 million radio receivers – or two for every person in the United States. Most stations concentrate on music and, in recent years, the main growth in sales has been in portable and car radios.

Above: A newspaper and magazine stand.

Below left: Newspapers published in New York include some in Spanish for Hispanic Americans. *USA Today* is published in several regional centres.

Below: Some magazines for young people cover such topics as sport and music. Others feature cartoons, some of which are comic while others, such as Superman and the Conan Saga, tell stories.

Below: Some of the magazines published in the United States are available throughout the English-speaking world.

The main source of news for most people is television. In 1991, there were 215 million TV sets throughout the United States and, on average, a television set in use in each home for seven hours a day. There are five main national television networks and 46 national cable networks. In 1992, more than 9,200 commercial and 1,200 non-commercial stations were operating in the United States.

Most TV stations are financed by advertising. There is, however, also a Public Broadcasting Service, funded by public donations, businesses, foundations and government grants.

Nine out of every ten viewers can choose from at least four channels, while 47 per cent have a choice of 11 channels. There are also cable networks, and many people in large cities have dozens of channels to choose from. Some channels broadcast only religious programmes – a reflection of the fact that about three out of every five Americans are church members.

Above: A disc jockey at a radio station.

Below: The *TV Guide* is one of the top magazines in the United States.

Fact file: home life and leisure

Key facts

Population composition: In 1989, people under 15 years of age made up 21.7 per cent of the population; people between 15 and 59 made up 61.4 per cent; and people of 60 and over made up 16.9 per cent. Women formed 51.25 per cent of the population.

Average life expectancy at birth: 76 years in 1990, as compared with 71 years in 1971 and 54 in 1920. (By comparison, people in Mexico live, on average, 70 years and people in India 59 years.) In 1990, women had an average life expectancy of 80 years as compared with 74 years in 1965. Women live, on average, seven years longer than men.

Rate of population increase (1980–90): 0.9 per cent per year (as compared with 1.0 per cent in 1965–80). A forecast of an annual rate of 0.8 per cent per year between 1990 and 2000 would give the United States a population of 270 million in the year 2000.

Family life (1990): The average age of people at their first marriage was 23.9 years (women) and 26.1 years (men). The average size of households was 2.63 persons. (The number of people living alone rose from 10.9 million in 1970 to 24.6 million in 1990.)

Homes: About 64 per cent of homes in 1990 were owner-occupied and 36 per cent were rented. The average annual income per household is $35,700 (1990, when £1.00 equalled $1.64).

Work: The total workforce in 1990 was 126,424,000, of which women formed 44.8 per cent. Unemployment in the civilian workforce stood at 5.4 per cent. Trade union membership in the total workforce in 1989 stood at 16.4 per cent.

Prices: In 1980–90, the average annual inflation rate was 3.7 per cent, as compared with 6.5 per cent in 1965–80.

Religions: Church membership in 1989 totalled 147,607,000. Protestants (including Baptists, Methodists, Lutherans, Episcopalians and Presbyterians) numbered 79 million, Roman Catholics 57 million, Jews 5.9 million, and Eastern Christian Churches 4.1 million.

▷ **How many households owned goods in 1990**

Most American households are well equipped with labour-saving devices.

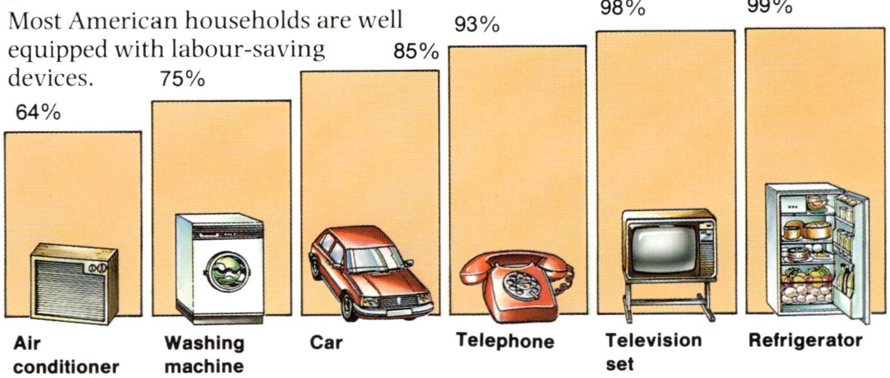

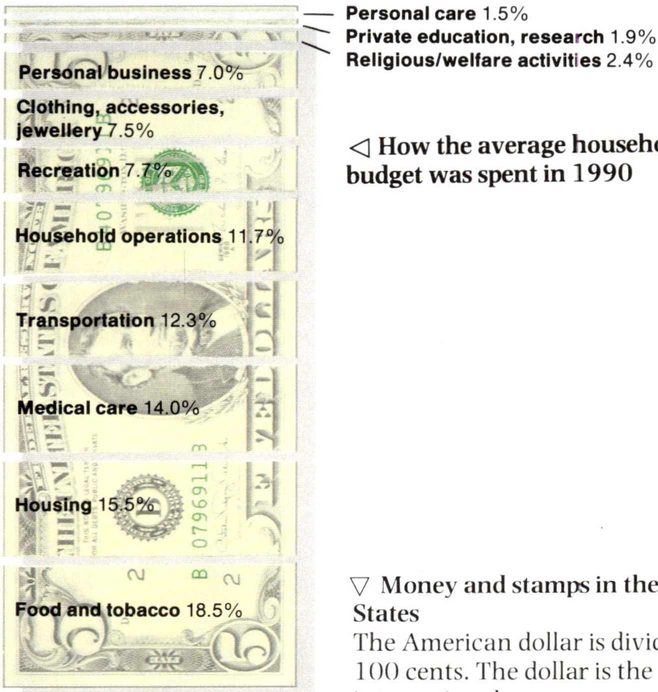

◁ **How the average household budget was spent in 1990**

▽ **Money and stamps in the United States**

The American dollar is divided into 100 cents. The dollar is the leading international currency.

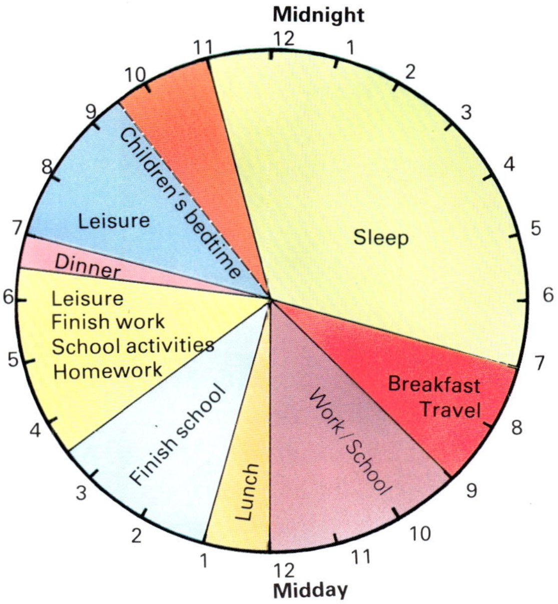

△ How the average family spends the day

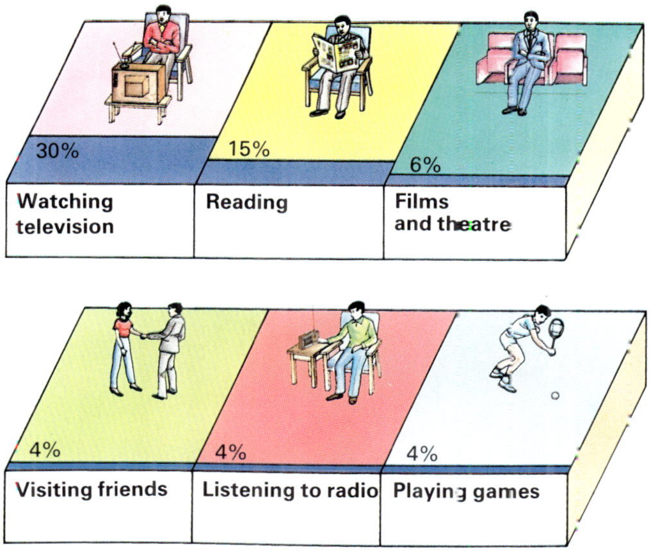

△ How often popular leisure pursuits were done in 1986

▽ Major holidays in the United States

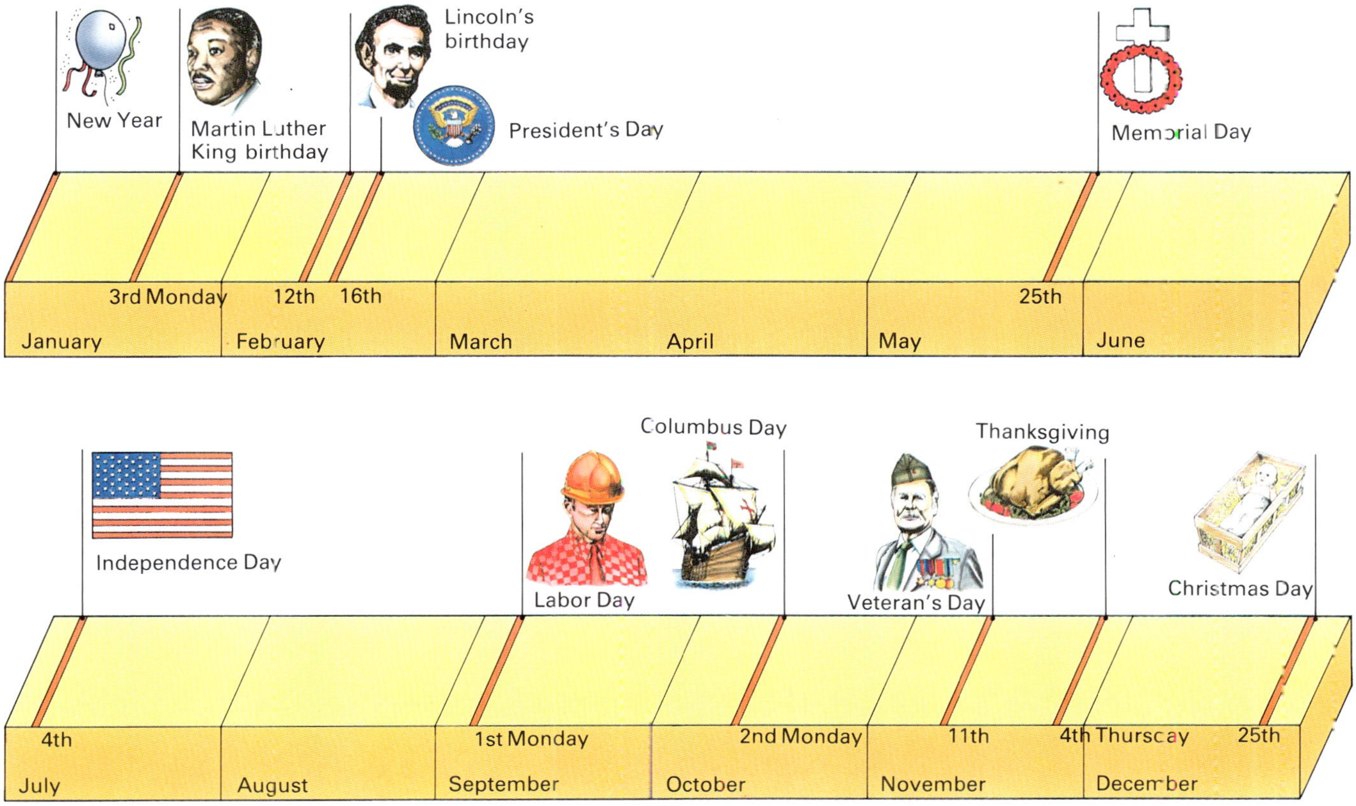

Farming and fishing

The United States is the world's leading producer of agricultural products, although farming accounts for only two per cent of the country's gross national product (the value of all goods and services produced). Not only does it produce enough food for its own needs, but it also accounts for a sixth of the world's food exports. Farming is so highly mechanized and scientific that farming, forestry and fishing together employ only about 3 per cent of the workforce (it was 15 per cent in 1950).

About 43 per cent of the land is farmed, with 43.4 per cent of the farmland being mainly devoted to crops, 52.6 per cent to livestock, and the rest to mixed farming. The average size of a farm is 186 ha (462 acres). Farms range in size from small plots of a few hectares to huge farms owned by business corporations. The corporate farms use the most advanced scientific techniques and farm machinery suitable for large-scale production.

Above: Many farms in the United States are large and highly mechanized. They employ comparatively few workers.

Right: Peanuts are harvested by cutting through the roots of the plants and lifting them from the soil. The United States is the third largest producer of peanuts.

The United States leads the world in the production of several items, including beef, cheese, maize (corn), poultry and soya beans.

Major farming regions include the Corn Belt, south and west of the Great Lakes, where maize, soya beans, lucerne (alfalfa) and pigs are important products. The Wheat Belt lies west of the Corn Belt. California grows citrus fruits, grapes for making wine, and rice, while the subtropical southeast also produces citrus fruits and rice as well as cotton, peanuts, sugar cane and tobacco. Forestry is especially important in the northwest, where Washington and Oregon produce about a quarter of the country's timber requirements.

Vast cattle ranches are located on the prairies and in the western states. Beef is also produced in the Midwest and South. The main dairy cattle region extends south of the Great Lakes from Minnesota to the state of New York.

Fishing is a major industry in the Gulf of Mexico and along the coasts. The chief commercial species caught are salmon, crabs, shrimps, tuna, menhaden, cod and flounders.

Above: Beef cattle are the most valuable farm product in the United States. These stockyards are in Oklahoma. Only Texas, Nebraska and Kansas have more beef cattle than Oklahoma.

Below: Red snappers are landed from a fishing boat in San Francisco harbour. California is the third most important fishing state after Louisiana and Alaska.

Natural resources

The United States is rich in resources. It has abundant sources of energy. It leads the world in the production of coal and uranium, which is used to fuel nuclear power stations. The United States is the second largest producer of crude oil and natural gas, after the former Soviet Union. Its oil reserves are among the world's largest.

Water is another major resource. Many of the country's rivers have been dammed to provide reservoirs of water for homes and industry, and for irrigation on farms. Hydroelectric power stations at the dams generate cheap electricity.

Most metallic and nonmetallic minerals are mined in the United States. For example, the country is among the world's top producers of asbestos products, copper, gold, gypsum, iron ore, kaolin (china clay), lead, phosphates, silver, sulphur and zinc. Bauxite is imported, although the United States leads the world in extracting aluminium from this ore. Other imported minerals include chromite, nickel, manganese and tungsten.

Above: Engineers drill for oil in Oklahoma, the fifth most important oil-producing state, after Texas, Alaska, Lousiana and California.

Left: Bingham Canyon Copper Pit, near Salt Lake City, Utah, is the world's largest opencast copper mine. It is 3.7 km (2.3 miles) across at its widest point. It is nearly 800 m (0.5 miles) deep.

The United States has large tracts of fertile soil. But much damage was done in the early days of European settlement, when pioneers cut down the forests in the east and grazed and ploughed the dry Great Plains. Over-intensive farming, overgrazing and deforestation resulted in soil erosion. In the 1930s, experts estimated that as much as 60 per cent of the land had been affected. Parts of the Great Plains, stripped bare of their grass, suffered prolonged droughts. The dry soil crumbled and was blown away by the wind, creating a huge, infertile "Dust Bowl". In the forested Appalachian Mountain region, so many trees were felled that the rain washed the exposed soil into the rivers.

Since the 1930s, farmers have learned to use scientific methods to conserve the soil. The Dust Bowl is now being farmed again, and trees have been planted on the steep slopes of the Appalachians. And a government agency, the Tennessee Valley Authority (TVA), has built dams to prevent flooding downriver.

Above: Cleveland, Ohio, on the south shore of Lake Erie, is a major steel and motor vehicle producing centre. Only Indiana produces more steel than Ohio among the states of the United States.

Below: The Grand Coulee Dam in the state of Washington is the greatest single source of water power in the United States. The water in the lake behind the dam is used to irrigate farmland.

Industry and trade

Although it has only five per cent of the world's population, the United States, the world's greatest industrial nation, accounts for more than a quarter of the total value of the world's goods and services. Industry contributes 29 per cent of the country's gross domestic product and employs 18 per cent of its workforce. Major manufactures include nonelectric machinery, transportation equipment, food products, textile products, chemicals, electrical and electronic machinery and equipment, metal products, metals, printed materials and paper products. The top manufacturing states are California, with its modern high-technology industries, New York, Ohio, Illinois, Michigan, Texas and Pennsylvania.

The United States has pioneered many industrial techniques aimed at producing the greatest number of goods at the lowest cost. In recent times, industry has been changing – and employing fewer workers – because of increasing use of automation and computers.

Above: The United States has been in the forefront in developing space technology.

Below: Seattle, the largest city in the state of Washington, is the home of the Boeing aircraft company.

Left: These new cars were produced on the assembly lines of the Chrysler Corporation, whose headquarters are in Detroit.

Below: *Star Wars* (1977) was one of the most successful movies of all time. The United States has some of the world's largest entertainment industries.

Between 1965 and 1990, the percentage of workers in service industries rose from 60 to 79 per cent. Services include banking and insurance, retail selling, health care, education and marketing, including advertising, a major industry in the United States. The wholesale and retail businesses alone employ about a fifth of the workforce.

The United States also plays a leading role in international trade, and the value of its exports and imports is greater than that of any other nation. The country's leading trading partners are Canada, Japan, Mexico, Germany, Britain and Taiwan. Major exports include machinery, transportation equipment, chemicals and food products. The United States also imports many materials, including metal ores and oil, and manufactures. In 1970, rises in world oil prices caused economic problems in the United States, which led to unemployment. Unemployment also resulted from competition with developing nations, such as South Korea, which have lower labour costs than the United States.

Transportation

Above: Road transport is the most important form of passenger transport in the United States.

The United States is such a vast country that transcontinental transportation services had to be built before the nation could be truly united.

Today the most important routes are country and urban roads and turnpikes, and freeways or expressways, with or without tollgates. Most passenger travel is by road, while about a quarter of the nation's freight traffic also goes by road. Bus services are excellent and there are two major networks: Greyhound and Continental Trailways. But most Americans travel by road in their own cars. In 1990, there were about 168 million licensed drivers and 193 million registered cars, buses and trucks.

Inland waterways handle about 15 per cent of the total freight traffic in the United States. The leading waterways are the Mississippi River system and the Great Lakes, which are linked to the Atlantic Ocean by the St. Lawrence Seaway. The chief seaports are New Orleans, New York City and Houston. In 1991, the United States had the eighth largest merchant fleet.

Below: A powerful truck transports cars.

Below right: Bus services criss-cross the country.

The United States has about 29 per cent of the world's railway track. Trains carry about a third of the freight traffic, but they are much less important in carrying passengers. However, some services are now being adapted for tourist travel in scenic areas. Some railway companies are independent, but most long-distance services are run by the National Railroad Passenger Corporation (Amtrak) and the Consolidated Rail Corporation (ConRail), two government-assisted bodies. Several cities have underground railways, as well as buses, trams and other services.

For passengers in a hurry, air transportation is excellent and relatively inexpensive. Airlines handle about 15 per cent of the passenger traffic. Those providing major domestic flights include American, Continental, Delta, Eastern, Northwest Orient, TWA, United, and Western. Chicago's O'Hare International Airport is one of the world's busiest – in 1989, a plane took off or landed, on average, every 40.4 seconds.

Above: Amtrak, which is officially called the National Railroad Passenger Corporation, operates most of the intercity passenger trains in the United States.

Below: Inland waterways, including the mighty Mississippi River, were once among the most important forms of transport in the United States.

Fact file: economy and trade

▷The distribution of economic activity in the United States

	Oil and natural gas		Citrus fruits
	Coal		Peanuts
	Iron ore		Tobacco
	Copper		Forest products
	Industry		Sugar
	Corn (maize)		Pigs
	Wheat		Beef cattle
	Soybeans		Dairy products
	Cotton		Fishing

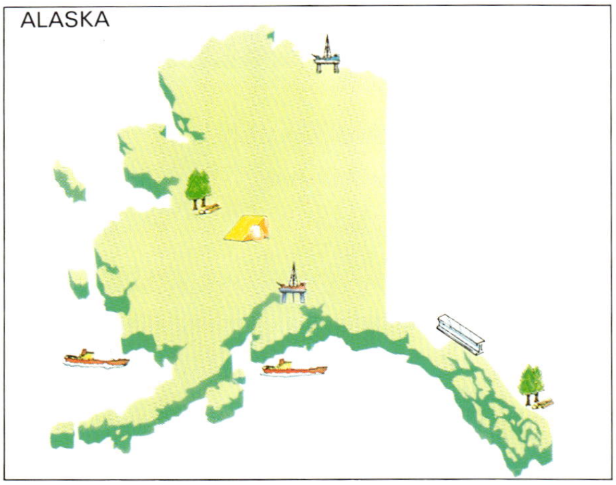

Key facts

Structure of production: Of the total gross domestic product (the GDP, or the value of all economic activity in the United States), farming, forestry and fishing contribute 2 per cent, industry 30 per cent and services 68 per cent.

Farming and forestry: The United States is the world's top farming nation; 43.2 per cent of the land is farmed. *Main products:* beef, milk, corn, soya beans, pork, wheat, cotton. *Livestock:* 99,337,000 cattle; 53,852,000 pigs; 10,745,000 sheep. Forests cover nearly a third of the land.

Fishing: The United States is the fourth leading fishing nation.

Mining: The United States is the world's second leading producer of coal, oil and natural gas. Also important are copper, gold, iron ore, silver, uranium and zinc.

Energy: Of the total electricity production in 1990, generators powered by coal, oil and natural gas accounted for 83.1 per cent, hydroelectric power stations for 4.3 per cent, and nuclear power stations for 9.2 per cent, and other sources 3.4 per cent.

Manufacturing: The United States is the world's leading manufacturing nation.

Trade (1990): *Total imports:* $494, 903 million; *exports:* $375,454 million. The United States is the world's leading trading nation.

Economic growth: The average real growth rate of the gross national product (GNP) between 1980 and 1990 was 2.2 per cent per year.

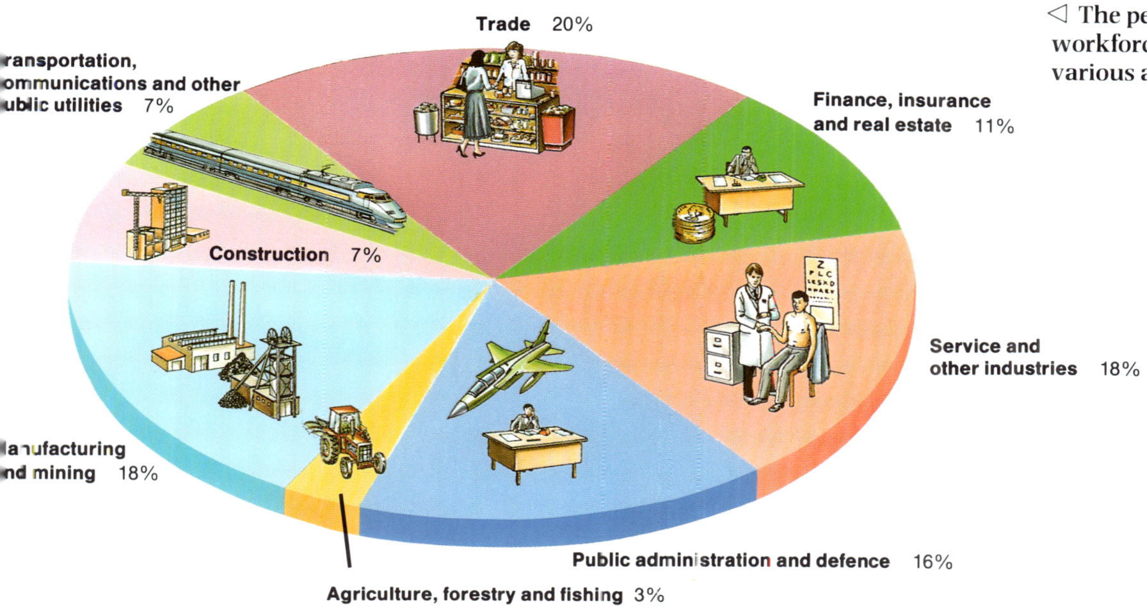

◁ The percentages of the workforce engaged in various activities

▷ **The USA's main trading partners, 1990**
The three leading trading areas for the United States are Japan and the rest of Asia, Canada and other countries in the Americas, and Western Europe.

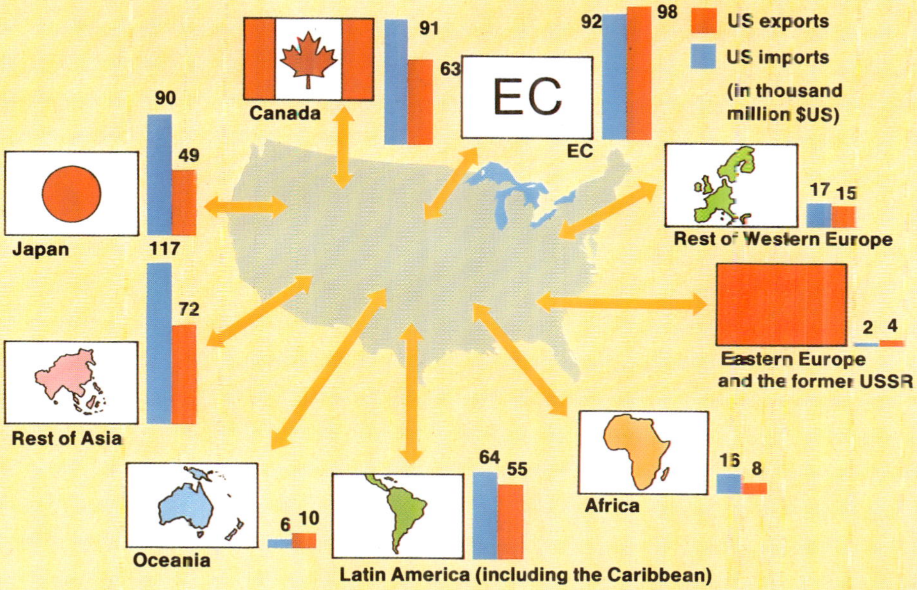

▽ **The composition of US imports and exports, 1990**
Manufactured products dominate the exports of the United States.

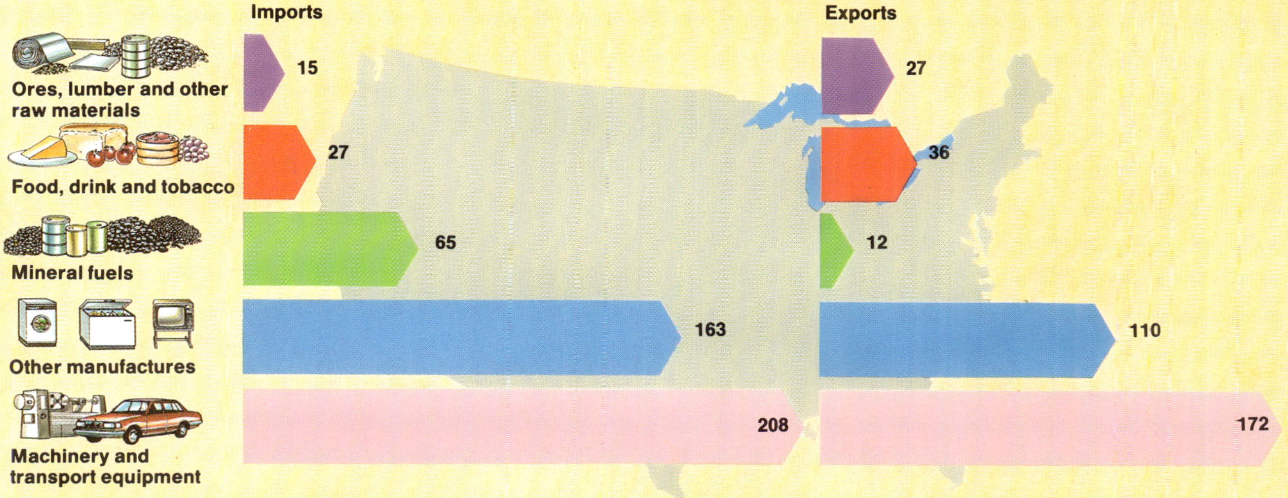

Education

Most Americans believe that they can improve their social and domestic status through education. As a result, over the last hundred years, young people have spent, on average, more time in school. For example, most children left school at the age of 13 or 14 in the early years of the 20th century. By 1940, most young people stayed on until the age of 18. Today, the average school-leaving age is still rising. About 30 per cent of people aged 18 to 24 are enrolled in colleges and universities.

All institutions of learning that receive government funding are racially integrated. Elementary and secondary education is mostly run by the individual states, and their systems differ, although generally all provide 12 years of free and compulsory education, with kindergarten for five-year-olds. More than 80 per cent of the elementary and high schools provide free education. But religious organizations and other private groups run some schools and about half of the institutions of higher education. Many students take part-time jobs to finance their higher education.

Above: Pre-school education (nursery schools and kindergartens) is generally for children of 5 years of age or younger. Children of 6 to 12 or 14 attend elementary schools.

Below: A classroom in New York. Systems of education vary from state to state. As a result, some schools have 6 and some 8 years (or grades) of elementary education.

Left: These schoolchildren live in the district of Harlem in New York City.

Below: Harvard University, Massachusetts, was founded in 1636, 16 years after the Pilgrims had founded Plymouth Colony, the second permanent British settlement in North America after Jamestown, Virginia.

The pattern of education varies, but there are three main systems. One starts with kindergarten, followed by six years (grades) of elementary school, three years at junior high school and three years at senior high school. Another consists of kindergarten, then eight years of elementary school and four years of high school. A third system consists of kindergarten, followed by six years (grades) of elementary school and six years of high school. High school graduation generally takes place at 17 or 18 years of age.

Higher education is provided by colleges, vocational schools and universities. Some of the country's major universities, including Harvard, Yale and Princeton, are famous throughout the world.

Adult education is especially important today. Many adults study to improve job skills, while others enrol for training to do jobs in new, high-technology industries.

The arts

In the late 19th century, a unique form of music, jazz, developed from the music of the black people of the United States. Early forms included ragtime and blues, and early exponents were W. C. Handy (1873–1958) and Louis Armstrong (1900–1971). Later jazz greats include the composer Duke Ellington (1899–1974) and Dizzy Gillespie (1917–).

The art of motion picture making was developed to a great extent in the United States. In the early 20th century, cinema was regarded as cheap entertainment. But the medium was given artistic form by the American D. W. Griffith (1875–1948), who directed *The Birth of a Nation* (1915) and *Intolerance* (1916) – films that influenced film-makers throughout the world. American films dominated a 1982 list of all-time best films, which was headed by *Citizen Kane* (1941), directed by Orson Welles (1915–1985). Since the 1950s, however, cinema audiences have declined because of competition from television.

Above: Louis Armstrong was the best-known of all jazz musicians.

Below left: *Citizen Kane*, made by and starring Orson Welles, is rated by many as the best movie of all time.

Below: *West Side Story* is a dynamic musical based on *Romeo and Juliet*. Most of the great American musicals are the result of collaboration between a group of artists.

The United States has made major contributions to more traditional art forms. Great writers have included novelists Herman Melville (1819–1891), author of *Moby Dick*, and Mark Twain (1855–1910), author of *The Adventures of Huckleberry Finn*, poets Walt Whitman (1819–1892) and Emily Dickinson (1830–1886), and dramatists Eugene O'Neill (1888–1953) and Arthur Miller (1915–). A special form of theatre is the musical. For example, the composer Leonard Bernstein (1918–1990) worked with playwright Arthur Laurents (1918–) and lyric-writer Stephen Sondheim (1930–) to create *West Side Story* (1957).

Concert music has been written by such composers as Aaron Copland (1900–1990) and Charles Ives (1874–1954), who is known for his experimental and uniquely American music. Major painters have included Charles Marion Russell (1864–1926), who depicted cowboy life, and Jackson Pollock (1912–1956), who is known for his abstract works.

Above: This scene from a film version of Mark Twain's masterpiece *The Adventures of Huckleberry Finn* shows Huck and a runaway slave, Jim, who travel together down the Mississippi River. Mark Twain was the pen name of Samuel Langhorne Clemens.

Below: The Lincoln Center for the Performing Arts is a handsome group of buildings, which house some of New York City's leading musical activities, including the Metropolitan Opera, the New York City Ballet and the New York Philharmonic.

The making of the modern United States

Above: On July 4, 1776, delegates from Britain's North American colonies adopted the Declaration of Independence.

Below: The Battle of Gettysburg was fought in 1863 during the Civil War, which stopped the country dividing into two parts.

The Revolutionary War, which began in 1775, ended in victory for the colonists in 1781, although the war did not officially end until the signing of the Treaty of Paris in 1783.

In the early 19th century, the United States gradually extended its control westward. In the Mexican War (1846–1848), the country gained vast areas in the West. However, progress was interrupted by the Civil War (1861–1865). This bitter conflict was fought on the issue of the right of the South to secede and to continue slavery. The victory of the North ensured the continuing unity of the country and the abolition of slavery.

In the late 19th century, industries were set up in the cities, utilizing the country's huge resources and fast increasing workforce of new immigrants. With tremendous energy, inventive skill and business genius, the people set out to make the United States the world's most powerful nation.

Above left: The Japanese made a surprise attack on the US naval base at Pearl Harbor in 1941. This led the United States to enter World War II.

Above: American troops took part in the invasion of Europe in June 1944.
Below: US troops assisted South Vietnam in a war against Communist forces.

When World War I broke out in Europe in 1914, many Americans felt that it was not their business. But in 1917, the United States entered the war and helped to bring it to an end a year later. The United States also entered World War II (which had begun in 1939) after a Japanese attack on their naval base at Pearl Harbor, Hawaii, on December 7, 1941. During the war, a team of international scientists in the United States developed the atomic bomb, which was dropped on Japan to bring an end to the war in 1945.

After the war, the United States was one of the world's two superpowers. The other, the Soviet Union, became a rival because of its Communist policies. The United States joined western defence alliances, such as the North Atlantic Treaty Organization. When Communist North Korea attacked South Korea in 1950, American troops aided the South. In the 1960s, the United States became involved in another Asian war, opposing Communist forces in South Vietnam. But in 1973, all American troops were withdrawn.

The United States today

As the leader of the Western Alliance, the United States still faces many challenges in foreign affairs. In the 1980s, it was increasingly concerned about unrest in Central America and the emergence there of left-wing groups, such as the Sandinista government of Nicaragua, which is backed by Communist Cuba. Also in the 1980s, the United States increased its military strength. But the ending of Communist rule in the Soviet Union and Eastern Europe led to cuts in nuclear weaponry.

At home, the 1970s and 1980s were marked by periodic economic recessions. Social problems included unemployment, crime and drug addiction, especially in the decaying inner cities. Among the many other challenges faced by American society was a general increase in the average age. In 1950, only four per cent of the population was 65 years or older. By 1990, this percentage had risen to 12 per cent.

Above: As a superpower, the United States acts as a policeman in various disputes, such as the Gulf War in the 1980s.

Below: A Republican Party convention held in Dallas, Texas, demonstrates the strength of democracy in the United States.

The United States faces its many problems with confidence. Its advanced technology, which has put astronauts on the Moon, remains supreme. And in tackling social problems and the political difficulties that arise from them, its strength lies in its democratic system. Not even the President is above criticism. The United States is also a country that has often led the world in formulating new ideas. In recent years, it has launched research on pollution of the environment and has passed many laws to control it, though much remains to be done.

The United States has evolved from a pioneering, agricultural society into the world's most powerful industrial nation. It is now entering a new phase, as job opportunities in industry decline because of new technology. The industrial cities are no longer the only magnets for the talented and ambitious. Instead, an increasing number of businesses are moving away from the cities, and many people are moving to more rural areas, where they can enjoy the natural beauty and tranquility.

Above: Bill Clinton, seen here with his wife Hillary and daughter Chelsea, defeated George Bush in the presidential elections in 1992.

Below: Despite the many problems faced by the United States at home and abroad, young Americans look forward to the future with confidence.

Fact file: government and world role

The States of the United States

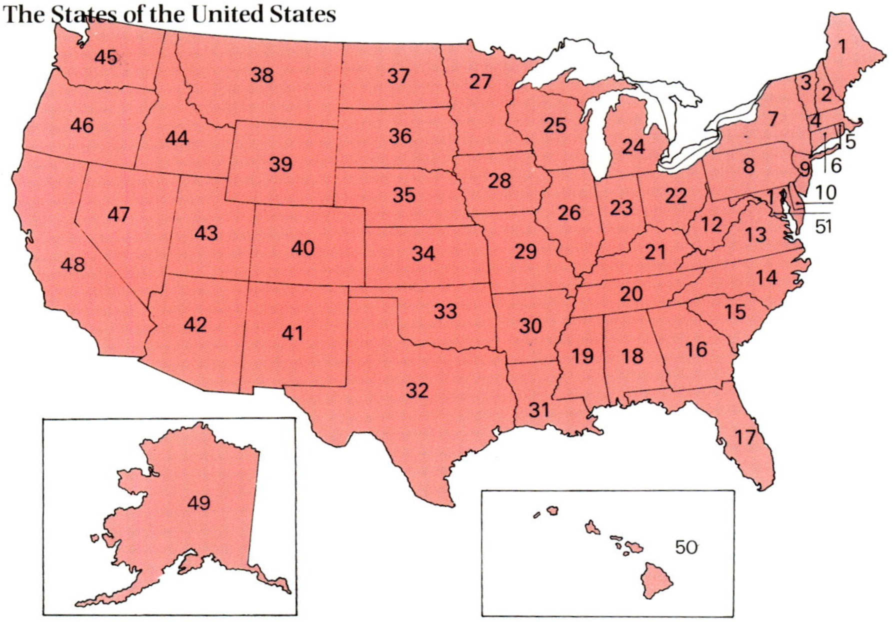

1 Maine
2 New Hampshire
3 Vermont
4 Massachusetts
5 Rhode Island
6 Connecticut
7 New York
8 Pennsylvania
9 New Jersey
10 Delaware
11 Maryland
12 West Virginia
13 Virginia
14 North Carolina
15 South Carolina
16 Georgia
17 Florida
18 Alabama
19 Mississippi
20 Tennessee
21 Kentucky
22 Ohio
23 Indiana
24 Michigan
25 Wisconsin
26 Illinois
27 Minnesota
28 Iowa
29 Missouri
30 Arkansas
31 Louisiana
32 Texas
33 Oklahoma
34 Kansas
35 Nebraska
36 South Dakota
37 North Dakota
38 Montana
39 Wyoming
40 Colorado
41 New Mexico
42 Arizona
43 Utah
44 Idaho
45 Washington
46 Oregon
47 Nevada
48 California
49 Alaska
50 Hawaii
51 Washington D.C.

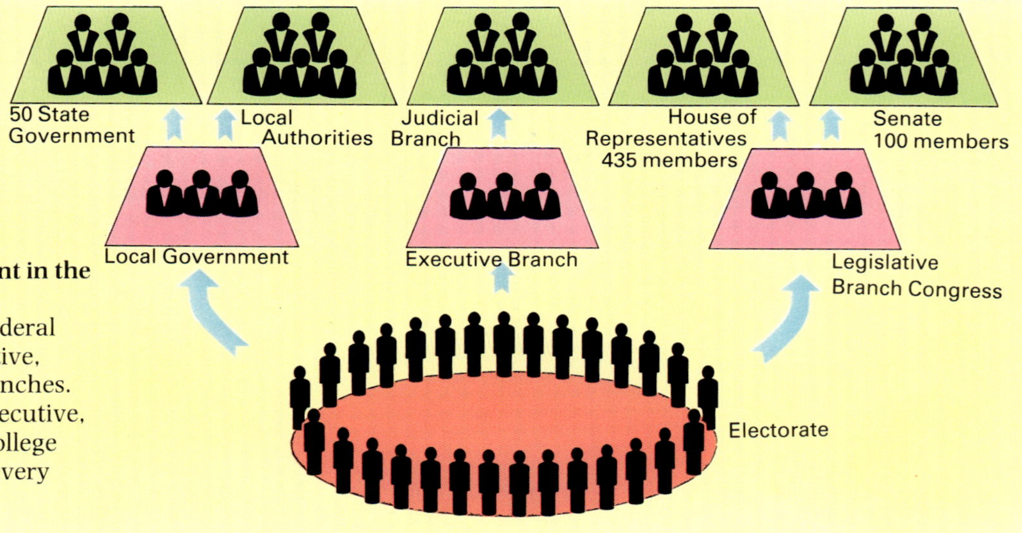

▷ **The system of government in the United States**
The chief elements of the federal government are the Executive, Legislative and Judicial branches. The President, the Chief Executive, is elected by an Electoral College chosen by all adult voters every four years.

Key facts

Official name: United States of America.
National anthem: The Star-spangled Banner.
National government: The United States is a federal republic. The federal government consists of three branches: executive, legislative and judicial. The Executive branch is represented by the President, who is the Chief Executive, Head of State and Commander of the armed forces.
Local government: Each state has an elected Congress with two Houses (except Nebraska which has a single-chamber legislature). An elected Governor heads the executive branch (government) of each state.
Armed forces: Service is voluntary, although men must register when they reach the age of 18. This register exists in case of a national emergency. *Army:* 731,700 personnel; *Navy:* (including 194,000 Marines): 507,500; *Air Force:* 517,400.
Economic alliances: The United States belongs to the OECD (Organization for Economic Co-operation and Development), the Colombo Plan and the South Pacific Commission.
Political alliances: The United States is a member of the United Nations and it contributes 25 per cent of the organization's regular budget. It also belongs to: the North Atlantic Treaty Organization (NATO) and ANZUS (with Australia and New Zealand). The United States also belongs to the Organization of American States (OAS).

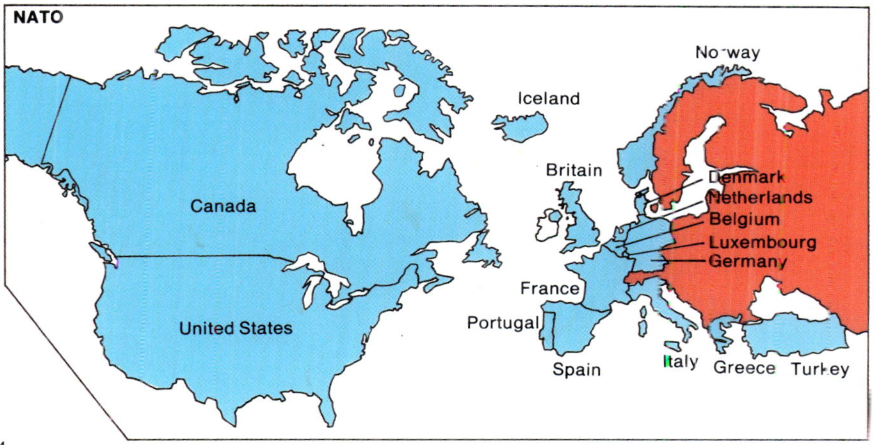

◁ **The World Role of the United States**
The United States works with its allies throughout the world. Especially important are such organizations as NATO and the Organization of American States. The adoption of a non-nuclear policy by New Zealand in the 1980s led to its suspension from ANZUS.

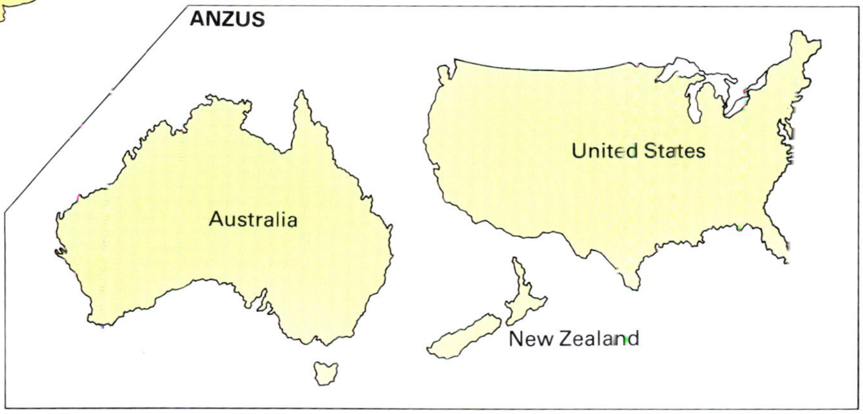

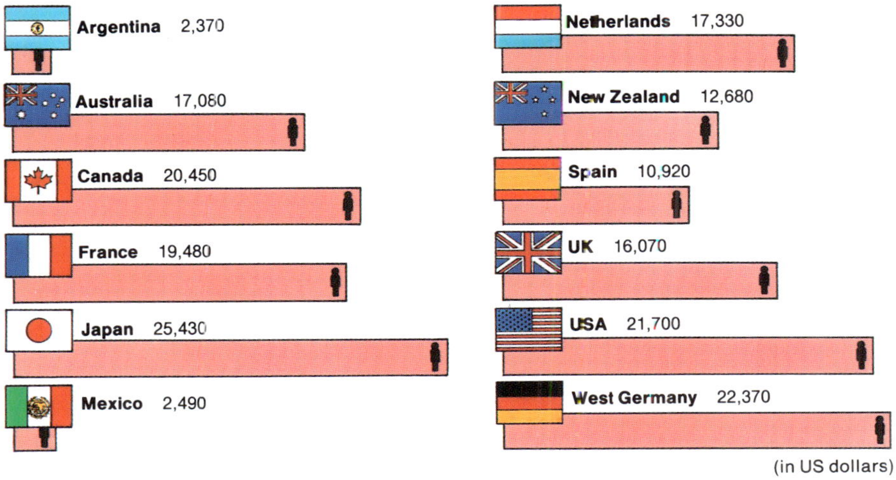

◁ **National wealth created per person in 1990**
The United States is the world's richest and most developed nation. Its gross national product (GNP) in 1990 was $5,445,825 million. This was more than 1.7 times the GNP of Japan and six times the GNP of the UK.

Index

PRINTED IN BELGIUM BY proost INTERNATIONAL BOOK PRODUCTION